T0193176

DICTIONARY
of
MUSICAL TERMS

To order additional copies of this book, contact:
Xlibris
844-714-8691
www.Xlibris.com
Orders@Xlibris.com

Book Designer: Rick Contreras
Art Director: Mike Nardone

ISBN: 978-1-4010-7238-4 (sc)

Print information available on the last page

Rev. date: 11/25/2020

Abbreviations, denoting the language in which the terms are written or from which they are derived:

F., French
I., Italian
G., German
Gk., Greek
L., Latin
S., Spanish

A. at, to by.

A CAPPELLA, literally in church style, unaccompanied vocial music.

ACCELERANDO, gradually faster.

ACCEL, gradually faster.

ACCENT, a slight stress placed upon a note to mark its place and relative impoertance in the bar.

ACCIACCATURA, (I) a species of arpeggio.

ACCIDENTALS, occasional sharps, flats, and naturals placed before notes in the piece.

ACOUSTICS, from the Greek denoting the science of sound.

ADAGIO, (I) very slow and expressive.

A DEUX, (F) for two instruments or voices.

'A DEUX, (F) for two hands.

AD LIBITUM, (L) at pleasure, at will. This expression implies that the time of some particular passage is left to the pleasure of the performer.

AD LIB. (L) same as AD LIBITUM

AFFRETTUOSO, affectionately.

AFFRETTANDO, hurrying, pressing onwards.

AFFRETT, same as AFFRETTANDO.

ADITATO, agitated (I) with agitation, anxiously.

AGREMENS, AGREMENTS (F) musical ornaments.

AIS, (G) note A sharp.

AL, ALL, ALLA, ALLO, (I) at the, to the, in the style of.

AL SEGNO, to (or at) the sign :S: a mark of repetition.

ALLA BREVE (L) this term is used to indicate a quick species of common time, formerly used in church music. Originally a time with four minum beats in each bar. Now usually applied to a time with two minim beats in each bar.

ALLA MARCIA, in march tsyle.

ALLA POLACCA, in the style of a polonaise.

ALL ARGANDO, broadening out; getting gradually slower, generally with an increase in tone.

ALLEGRETTO, (I) (lit. a little allegro) somewhat cheerful but slightly slower than allegro.

ALLEGRO, (I) lively, fast. A term implying a rapid and vivacious movement, but which is frequently notified by the addition of other words as:

ALLEGRO CON FUOCO, quick with fire.

ALTISSIMO, (I) extremely high as to pitch.

AMORE, love.

ANCORA, again, yet.

ANALYSE, (F) an analysis.

ANDANTE, (I) a slow and distinct movement.

ANDANTINO, (I) a little slower than andante.

ANIMA, CON

ANIMATO (I) with animation; in a spirited manner.

ANIMOSO SAME AS ANIMATO.

ANTHEM, a composition in the sacred style

ANTICIPATION, taking of a note or chord previous to its natural and expected place.

APPASSIONAYO, passionately.

A PIACERE, (I) at the pleasure of the performer.

A POCO PIU LENTO, (I) a little slower.

A POCO PIU MOSSO, (I) a little quicker.

APPOGGIATURA, (I) a note of embellishment (grace note)

ARCO, (lit. bow) in string music, a direction to the player to use the bow, not to pluck the strings (with the bow).

ARIA, (I) an air or song.

ARIOSO, (I) in the style of an air; vocal, melodious.

ARPEGGIANDO This word implies that the notes of a chord must be

ARPEGGIATO played in quick succession generally from lowest note

ARPEGGIO to the highest note.

ARTIST, (I) a virtuoso; a first-rate performer.

AS, (G) A flat.

ASSAI, very.

A TEMPO, (I) in time. A term used to denote that after a change in

A TEM., time, the performer must return to the original degree of movement.

ATTACCA, Go on atonce.

ATTACCA SUBITO, Go on at once

AUGMENTED, a term applied to such intervals as are more than major or perfect.

AU MOUVEMENT, (F) in time.

A UNA CORDA, (I) on one string.

AUSDRUCK, (G) expression.

AUXILIARY NOTES, a term applied to such notes as st and on the next degree of the stave above or below any principle note.

B, (G) B flat-H is B natural.

BALLAD, a short and familiar song.

BALLET, (F) a theatrical representation of some story or fable by means of dance or metrical action, accompanied with music.

BAR, lines drawn across the stave to divide the music in small and equal portions of duration; each of these small portions in themselves is also called a bar.

BARCAROLLE, (I) air sung by the VEnetian gondoliers, or boatmen while working. These melodies possess simple and artless beauty, delightful to the unpractised and also to the most cultivated ear.

BARITONE, a male voice, intermediate, in respect to pitch between the bass and the tenor voices.

BARRE, (F) a term used in playing guitar. It implies that a temporary nut is to be formed by means of the fore finger of the left hand.

BASS OR BASE, the lowest part in music.

BASSOON, a wind-instrument.

BATTUTA, (I) A bar; A beat.

BEAT, one of the principle graces in music.

BEBUNG, (G) Repetition of a note.

BECARRE, (F) natural sign (♮)

BEMOL, (F) flat sign. (♭)

BEMOLLE, (F) flat sign. (♭)

BEN, BENE, (I) well; as,.

BEN MARCATO, (I) well marked. This expression indicates that the passage must be executed in a clear, distinct, and strongly accented manner.

BEQUADRO, natural sign (♮)

BEWEGLICH, (G) with movement.

BEWEGT, (G) with movement.

BIS, (L) twice. A term which indicates that a certain passage distinguished by a curve draws over or under it must be performed twice; this abbreviations saves writing the passage over again.

BOGENSTRICK, (G) a stroke of the bow.

BOLERO, a Spanish dance with castenets in 3/4 time.

BOURREE, (F) a lively dance, in common time, beginning with an odd crotchet.

BOW, a round stick having little projections at each end to hold the hairs which form the effective part.

BRACES, curved or straight lines indicating that the notes which they connect are to be played or sung together.

BRAVURA, CON, (I) with vigor, with boldness (dash and brilliancy).

BREIT, (G) broad.

BRIDGE, that part of a stringed instrument over which the strings are drawn.

BRILLANTE, brilliant.

BRIO, vigour.

BRIOSO, vigorously.

CADENCE, a close in melody or harmony. An ornamental and extemporaneous passage introduced at the close of a piece of music.

CALANDO, gradually slower and softer.

CALMANDO, calming.

CALMATO, calmed.

CANON, a species of uninterrupted imitation.

CANTABILE, (I) in a melodious, graceful, and singing style.

CANTANDO, (I) this word, placed over a piano-forte passage indicates that the sounds must be blended softly into each other as in singing.

CANTANTE, (I) a part which is intended for the voice.

CANTATA, (I) a species of composition for one voice, consisting of an intermixture of air and recitative.

CANTILENA, a piece in the style of a song.

CANTO FERMO, (I) a chant or melody; as also any subject consisting of a few long, plain notes, given
as a theme for counterpoint.

CANZONE, (I) an air in two or three parts.

CANZONELTA, (I) a short canzone, or song.

CAPRICE, (F) a fanciful and irregular species of composition.

CAPO, (lit. head) the beginning.

CAPPELLA, church (see a cappella.)

CAPRICCIOSO, in a fanciful style.

CAROL, the name applied to the old ballads sung at Christmas by itinerant minstrels.

CASTAGNETS, OR CASTANETS, hollow shells used to accompany dance tunes in Spain and other southern countries.

CAVATINA, (I) an air of one movement or part only, occasionally preceded by a recitative.

CADEZ, (R) gradually relax the speed.

CELERITA, speed.

CES, (G) the note C flat.

C. F., see Canto Fermo.

CHANSON, (F) a song.

CHANT, (F) a song or melody, the vocal part.

CHORAL, (G) a psalm tune.

CHORD, a combination of several sounds forming harmony.

CHOROUS, a band or company of singers.

CHROMATIC, proceeding by semitones, or formed by means of semitones.

CINQUE, a composition intended for five voices.

CIS, (G) the note C sharp.

CLAVICHORD, a small keyed instrument of the spinet kind.

CLARINET, a wind-instrument blown with a reed.

CLAVIER, (F. G.) the key board of a piano or organ.

CLEFS, the signs (𝄞) (𝄢) (𝄡) are called clefs. The clefs are placed at the beginning of the staff, and fixes the letter name of the line on which it is written. The three clefs "G," "F," "C," fixes the position of the notes G, F, and C, on the staff.

CLEF DE FA, (F) the F, or bass clef.

CLEF DE SOL, (F) the G. or treble cleff.

CLEF D'UT, (F) the C clef.

CODA, a few bars added at the close of a composition beyond its natural termination.

COL, COLL, COLLA, COLLO, (I) with the.

COL LEGNO, (lit, with the wood) in string music, a direction to play with the wood of the bow.

COLLA PARTE, (lit. with the part), COLLA VOCE (lit. with the voice) a direction to the accompanist to follow the solo instrument or voice.

COME, as.

COME PRIMA, as at first.

COME SOPRA, as above.

COMODO, COMMODO, CON, (I) quietly (easily) with composure.

COMMON CHORD, a chord consisting of a bass note together with its third and fifth, to which the octave is often added.

COMMON TIMES, those which have an even number of parts in a bar.

COMPASS, the range of notes that the voice or instrument are capable of producing.

COMPOSITION, any musical production is so called. The art of inventing music.

COMPOUND INTERVALS, such as exceed the extent of an ocatve.

COMPOUND TIMES, those measures which contain two or three principal accents, as, 6/8, 12/8, 9/8, 9/4, etc.

CON, (I) with.

C

CON ANIMA, (I) with animation and feeling.

CON ESPRESSIONE, (I) with expression.

CON FUOCO, with fire (animation).

CON GRAZIA, with grace (elegance).

CON MOTO, with agitated expression.

CON SORDINI, (I) with mute.

CON SPIRITO, (I) with spirit.

CONCERT, a musical performance of some length.

CONCERTO, a composition in which the solo instrument displays the virtuoso skills against an orchestral accompaniment (usually in three movements.)

CONCORD, combinations of agreeable sounds.

CONDUCTOR, a person who directs several players or groups (orchestra, choral groups) in performance.

CONSECUTIVE, a term applied to similar intervals succeeding one another in a regular order.

CONSERVATOIRE, a school of music.

CONSONENT, parts that harmonize well with each other.

CONSONANCE, intervals pleasing to the ear.

CONTRA-BASSO, (I) the double bass.

CONTRA-FAGOTTO, a double bassoon.

CONTRALTO, (I) a counter-tenor voice. The lowest species of female voices and the highest of male voices.

CONTRAPUNTAL, (I) music that is written according to the rules of strict counterpoint.

CONTRARY MOTION, the movement of parts in opposite directions.

CONTRA, (I) low, under, against (an octave lower).

CORDA, (I) CORDE, (F) a string; as sopra una corda, on one string.

COTILLON, a French lively dance in 6/8 time.

COUNTERPOINT, (point against point), part against part. The art of combing melodies-adding one or more parts to a given theme or subject. The term counterpoint also means the added melody, part. (note against note)

CRESCENDO, CRESC, CRES, gradually louder

CROTCHET, a note half the value of the minim. In America the quarter-note.

DA, (I) by, for, from.

DA CAPO, (I) D. C., from the beginning.

DA CAPO, AL FINE, (I) an expression placed at the end of the movement, directing performer to return to first part, and end where the word fine is placed.

DAL, (I) by, as.

DAL SEGNO, (I) from the sign, a mark of repetition.

DECISO, decisively.

DECRESCENDO, (I) gradually softer.

DEGREE, the interval between any adjacent notes on the stave.

DELIBERATO, deliberate.

DELICATO, (I) delicately.

DEMI, (F) a half.

DEMI-CADENCE, a half cadence in harmony.

DEMI-SEMI-QUAVER, (I) a note half the value of a semiquaver. The American thirty-second note.

DES, (G) D flat.

DESCENT, the lowering of the tone of a voice or instrument.

DESTRA, right.

DETACHE, (F) staccato.

DI, (I) of.

DIA, (GK) through.

DIAPASON, interval of an octave; also certain essential organ stops which extend throughout the whole scale of the instrument. (Ex. open diapason, stopped diapason, double diapason, etc.)

DIATONIC, (G) notes used according to the degrees of the major or minor scales, or by tones and semitones only.

DIMINISHED, less than perfect, applied to intervals, chords.

DIMINISHED INTERVALS, less than perfect or minor intervals by one semitone (half-step).

DIMINUENDO, DIM., gradually softer (⊳).

DERGE, a funeral song.

DIS, D sharp.

DISCORD, a dissonant combination of sounds.

DISPERSED HARMONY, harmony in which the notes, forming the different chords are separated from each other by wide intervals.

DISSONANCE, intervals or chords displeasing to the ear.

DISSONANT, a disagreeable combination of sounds.

DIVISI, (I) (Divided) in orchestral scores, means that the body of players playing in unison, octaves or other intervals divide into two or more parts, the number of parts being specified.

DOLCE, sweetly.

DOLCISSIMO, (DOLCISS), as sweetly as possible.

DOLENTE, sadly.

DOLORE, (I) sorrow (CON DOLORE, with grief).

DOMINANT, the fifth note of the scale.

DOPPIO, double.

DOPPIO MOVIMENTO, twice the speed.

DOT, when placed after a note or rest increases its value by half of its original duration.

DOUBLE TONGUEING, a method of articulating quick notes used in flute music and some brass instruments, etc.

DROIT, (F) right; as maine droit, right hand.

DUET, a composition for two, singers, players, etc.

DUO, see duet.

DUR, (G) Major (minor, moll).

DYNAMICS, the various degrees of sound.

E, ED, (I) and.

ECOSSAISE, (F) a dance originally from Scotland in 3/2 or 2/4 time. In modern form it is in quick 2/4 time.

ELEGY, a musical poem, sad and touching.

EIS, (G) E sharp.

EMBOUCHURE, the mouthpiece of a musical instrument. Example: flute, Bassoon, French horn, etc.

EMPHASIS, a stress or marked accent on any note.

EN ANIMANT (F) gradually faster.

EN DEHORS, (F) prominently.

EN PRESSANT, (F) hurrying.

EN RETENT, (F) gradually slower.

ENCORE, (again) the demand by audience at performances for repetition or further performance.

ENERGIA, energy (Energico - Energetic).

ENSEMBLE, (F) together. A term applied to music in parts, when the several performers unite to produce a perfect over all smoothness, as regards time and style-as to leave nothing further to be desired.

ENTR'ACTE, music played between the acts of the opera, play.

EQUIVOCAL, a term applied to such chords, as by a change in the notation, may belong to several keys.

EQUIVOCAL CHORD, that chord whose fundamental base is not indicated by the interval by which it is formed.

ES, E flat.

ESPRESSIVO, or (I) CON ESPRESSION, with expression.

EXPOSITION, is the statement, in the first part of a movement, of the musical subjects, upon which the whole movement is built. In the different forms, regulation of the rules are determined by the form used..

EL, (L) and.

ETUTE, a study, exercise, caprices.

EXPRESSION, a player is said to play with expression, when he carefully exercises judgement on matters of pitch, duration, tone (Example: forte, piano, leggato, staccato) and imparts to the composition his own feelings.

EXTREME, means intervals in an augmented state.

EXTEMPORISATION, (or improvisation) thinking and performing music unpremeditatedly.

FA, in solfaing the note F.

FACILE, easy.

FACILMENTE, with facility.

FAGOTTO, (I) bassoon.

FALSE RELATION, is a term used in harmony to denote certain harmonic progressions in which notes which have occured in one chord, occur again in the next, altered by a sharp or flat, but not in the very same part, in contradiction to the laws of harmony.

FALSETTO, notes above a man's natural voice range, which can only be produced artificially.

FANTASIE, (F) FANTASIA, (I) a unrestricted composition in which the composer gives himself up wholly to the fancy of his ideas.

FANDANGO, a lively Spanish dance in triple time usually with guitar and castanets.

FERMATA, pause.

FERMAMENTE, (I) with firmness and decision.

FES, F flat.

FEURIG, (G) fiery.

FIFTH, is a perfect comsonance (three whole tones and a semitone (half step).

FIGURE, a short succession of notes, in chords or melody which gives a complete impression.

FIGURED BASS, a bass having figures placed over the notes to indicate the harmony.

FINALE, last movement of a composition.

FINE, (I) the end.

FIS, (G) Fsharp.

FLAT, ($\flat$) the sign that lowers a note by a semitone (half stop).

FLAUTO, (I) flute.

FORM, music is arranged into phrases and sentences (through the relationship of pitch and thythm, use of repetition and contrast) which are organized into forms. Example: Waltz, Sonata, Rondo, Minuet, etc.

FLORED, ornamental, figured, embellished.

FLUTE, wind instrument (woodwind).

FORTE, F, loud.

FORTE-PIANO, the piano is so called because of its wide range of volume from piano (soft) to forte (loud).

FORTISSIMO, (I) very loud.

FORZANDO, (I) FORZ., note is marked with special emphasis or force.

FORZA, FORZATO (FZ), forced.

FOURTH, an interval of four degrees (two whole tones and a semitone).

FRENCH HORN, a wind instrument.

FRETS, the small projections fixed across the finger board that show where the notes are to be stopped. (guitar, mandolin, etc.)

FUGUE, a form of composition, based on a theme called the subject which is answered by other parts (voices) according to strict rulels. Earlier parts were called voices and this is still in use.

FULL SCORE, a complete score of all the parts of a composition instrumental, vocal or both combined.

FUNDAMENTAL BASS, a bass formed of the roots of chords only.

FUNDAMENTAL CHORD, a chord the lowest note of which is its root.

FUNEBRE, (F & I) funeral; as Marche Funebre, a funeral march.

FUOCO, CON (I) with fire.

FURORE, CON (I) with fury.

FURIOSO, furiously.

GAI, (G) gay.

GALOP, (G) a quick spirited dance in 2/4 time.

GAVOTTE, French dance in common time, beginning on third beat of the bar

GAUCHE, (F) left, main gauche, left hand.

GENERATING TONE, the principal tone caused by the vibration of stringed instruments when one tone is struck.

GES, (G) G flat.

GIGA, GIGUE, (F) (jig) a lively dance in 6/8 or 12/8 time.

GIOCOSO, gay, merry.

GIS, (G) G sharp.

GIUSTO, exact, strict.

GLISSANDO, (I) (sliding-in a gliding manner). A rapid succession of notes produced by gliding the tip of the finger along the surface of the piano keys, or across the strings of the harp. Also possible on a trombone, etc.

GLOCKENSPIEL, an instrument made of a series of tuned bells or steel bars which is played by one performer. Keyboard or wodden hammer, written two octaves below the actual pitch.

GONG, made of bronze; sounded with a bass drumstick. A round (eastern) instrument.

GRACES, name for the ornaments. The most usual are appoggiatura, accoaccatira, arpeggio, mordent, trill (shake) and turn, tremolo.

GRANDIOSO, (I) in a grand manner.

GRAND OPERA, a serious and continuous musical drama, sung throughout with orchestral accompaniment.

GRAVE, (I) a very slow and solemn movement.

GRAZIA, GRAZIOSO, (I) gracefully.

GREGORIAN MUSIC, a collection of ancient ecclesiastical music used in connection with services of the Roman Church ever since early Christian times.

The three musical dialects of the Western Church are: 1. Ambrosian Music. 2. Visigothic (Mozarabic). 3. Gregorian.

GREGORIAN TONES, eight groups of chants, corresponding to the eight modes.

GROSSE CAISSE & GROSSE TROMMEL, (F. G.) for bass drum.

GRUPPETTO, a group of notes, a turn.

GUITAR, a string instrument belonging to a family consisting also of the less familiar lutes and others.

GUSTO, GUSTOSO, (I) CON, with taste.

H, (G) B natural.

HALF-NOTE, a minim.

HARMONY, is the science of tone combinations and the art of using such combinations.

HARMONICS, a series of tones, whose vibration numbers, are in the ratio of 1: 2: 3:, etc., is called a harmonic series. Each of the separate tones of the series are called harmonics. The lowest tone of the series being the first harmonic (fundamental tone) the octave above being the second harmonic, etc. (Partial is the lowest term of the series—overtone is any one of the separate notes other than the lowest note.)

HARP, a stringed instrument consisting of a triangular frame having chords distended in parallel directions from the upper part to one of its sides. The harp has separate notes for sharps, flats and naturals, thus forming a true picture of the actual written sound.

HARPISCHORD, a keyed instrument that preceded the piano and was very popular during the 16th to 18th centuries. The instrument was not capable of dinamic change to tone. The strings were set in vibration by quill or leather points. The Harpischord's descent in principle came from the Psaltery as also the Pianoforte derived from the Dulcimer.

HAUTBOY, (E) HAUT-BOIS, (F) the oboe.

HIDDEN CONSECUTIVES, such as occur in passing by similar motion to two parts approaching the interval of a fifth or octave. From the 17th to 19th century the theorists forbade it.

HIS, (G) B sharp.

HORN, French horn, a brass instrument.

HORNPIPE, the name of an old dance in triple time. Modern tunes of this name are usually in common time.

HYMN, anciently a song in honor of the Gods or of heroes. In the present, it signifies a short, religious, lyric poem.

IL, (I) the.

IL CANTO, (I) the song.

IL PIU, (I) the most.

IMITATION, when a voice or part repeats a figure, melody (motive or phrase) previously heard in another voice. Imitation may be held to include every form of canon. In the classical period imitation preserved the rhythm and general outline only.

IMPERFECT CADENCE, a cadence where the dominant harmony is preceded by the common chord of the tonic.

IMPERFECT CONSONANCES, in harmony, a term applying to the Major and Minor thirds, and Major and Minor sixths.

IMPERFECT CONCORD, means all concords except the fourth and fifth.

IMPERFECT PERIOD, a termination that does not fully satisfy the ear.

IMPETUCSO, impetuously.

IMPROMPTU, an extemporaneous piece.

IN ALT, the notes from G, the space immediately above the treble stave up to the next F inclusive.

INCALZANDO, gradually louder and faster.

INSTRUMENTATION, (orchestration), the art of combining (and arranging) music for instruments (different timbres). This takes a thorough knowledge of ranges, capabilities, and harmony

INTERLUDE, something played in between parts of performances, church services, etc. A musical work.

INTERMEZZO, light and pleasing pieces usually introduced between acts to the Italian opera, etc., from the year 1500 on. Later used by composers as an independent piece of small dimension.

INTERVAL, the distance (or difference of pitch) between two notes. There are Major, Minor, perfect, diminished, and augmented intervals.

INTONATION. (1) the opening tones of a plain-song melody. (2) singing or playing in tune.

INTRODUCTION, a chord, motto theme or movement that leads up to the main subject matter or movements etc., or composition.

INVENTION, a small piece in two parts, each developing a single idea.

INVERSION, a change of position in respect to intervals and chords as arises from placing the upper notes at bottom and the bottom notes at above.

INVERTED COUNTERPOINT, counterpoint is called inverted when the parts are completely invertible (change places). The higher parts takes the lower part and the lower takes the higher. If the composition is in two parts it is called double counterpoint.

IRRESOLUTO, (I) irresolutely, hesitatingly.

ISTESSO TEMPO L, the same pace.

JIG, a quick movement in compound time of 6/8 or 12/8.

JOTA, a spanish dance dating from the 12th century similar to a waltz in three time, usually accompanied with guitar, cstanets, pandereto.

KEY, the lever by which the notes of a piano-forte, organ, etc., are made to sound. Flutes, oboes, and other wind instruments also have keys, by which certain holes are opened or shut. A key is also an assemblage of notes each of which has a fixed and distinct relation to one particular note which is called the key note (tonic).

KEY-BOARD, the row of keys of a piano-forte, organ, etc.

KEY-NOTE, the note by which the key is named.

KYRIE, (L) Lord. In the Catholic service the first movement of the mass begins with the words (music) "Kyrie eleison, Christ eleison, Lord have mercy upon us. Christ have mercy upon us.

L., L.H., left hand in piano-forte music.

LA, in solfaing used to the note A.

LA, (I and F) the.

LAGE, (G) position used. The positions in violin playing.

LANDLER, (G) LANDERER, Country dance or air in a rustic and popular style, usually in 3/8 time.

LANGSAM, (G) slowly.

LARGAMENTE, LARGHEZZA, (I) in a free, broad, full style.

LARGHETTO, (I) slow but less so than Largo.

LARGHISSIMO, (I) extremely slow.

LARGO, (I) slow and solemn (broad).

LAUT, (G) loud.

LAY, a light, fanciful song.

LE, (I) the; as.

LEBHAFT, (G) loud.

LEADING NOTE. the seventh note of the scale (of any key) and the seventh leads to the principal note (the tonic) by a semitone.

LEDGER LINES, LEGER LINES, extra short lines added above and below the staff for the notes beyond the staff range.

LEGATO, (I) connected. A word meaning the passage from note to note being connected and smooth.

LEGGIERO, lightly.

LEIT-MOTIV, (LEIT-MOTIF), (G) leading or guiding theme. A short figure (melodic phrase, themes, etc.) used recurringly to describe and associate certain ideas, persons or situations in a story, drama, etc.

LENTO, slow.

LEISE, (G) soft.

LIBRETTO, the text of an opera or oratorio.

LIEBLICH, (G) lovely.

L'ISTESSO MOVIMENTO, L'ISTESSO TEMPO, (I) in the same time as previous movement.

LOCO, in usual place reestablishes the actual pitch of notes after 8 vaalta, or 8 va bassa.

LOURE, (F) a dance usually in 6/4 time.

LUNGA PAUSO, (I) notifys the performer that he will cease playing for a considerable time.

LUSINGANDO, coaxing, flattering (in a soft tender manner).

LUTE, a large, beautiful stringed instrument of oriental origin which became known in the time of the Crusades.

LYRE, an ancient musical stringed instrument used among the Greeks.

LYRIC, LYRICAL, poetry adapted for and set to music.

M

MA, but.

MADRIGAL, (I) a secular composition for voices. (14th century originated in Italy).

MAESTOSO, magestically.

MAGGIORE, (I) the Major Key (Major).

MAJOR, greater in respect to intervals and modes. (Major is greater by half step than minor).

MAIN, (F) hand as Main Droite, M, D. right hand. Main gauche M. G. left hand.

MAIN DROIT, right hand.

MAIN GAUCHE, left hand.

MANCANDO, gradually softer.

MANDOLIN, a small and beautiful stringed instrument of the lute kind. The Mandolin is tuned like the violin, in fifths.

MANUAL, (G) the key-board.

MARCATO, MARC., marked.MARCH, a piece usually associated with military movements. A rhythmical and harmonised composition, written for a band of wind instruments, usually designed to accompany marching.

MARTELLATO, forcibly marked, hammered.

MARZIALE, martial.

MASS, a Catholic musical service, consisting of several movements.

MASSIG, (G) moderate.

MEASURE, the division of time by which the air and motion of the music is regulated.

MEDIANT, the third note of the scale.

MEDLEY, different parts or passage of well-known songs so arranged that the latter words of one part connects with the beginning of another song.

MELODY, a succession of single tones so arranged as to produce an agreeable effect on the ear.

MEN., MENFORT, (I) (MENO) abbreviation of meno, less.

MEN FORTE, (I) less loud.

MENO, less.

MESTO, sadly.

METRE, the rhythmical structure as concerned with the division into measures of time units (beats).

METRONOME, an instrument for the purpose of indicating the exact pace (tempo) the composer wishes to have his work performed.

MEZZO, (I) half.

MEZZO VOCE, (lit. half voice) in an undertone.

MEZZO FORTE, MF, moderately loud.

MEZZO PIANO, MP, moderately soft.

MEZZO STACCATO, half-staccato.

MEZZO SOPRANO, (I) a female voice lower in pitch than the soprano.

MINIM, the American half-note.

MINOR, less, in regards to intervals (1/2 step less than Major).

MINUET, a French dance, slow and graceful, in 3/4 time, sometimes beginning on the third, but mostly on the first beat. When used in concluding movements of overtures, sonatas, etc., it is usually a quick tempo and is marked "Scherzo".

MISTERIOSE, misterious.

MISERERE, (L) have mercy.

MIT, (G) with.

M.M., MAELZEL'S METRONOME, abbreviation for metronome.

MODERATO, in moderate time.

MODES, the ancient or medieval modes were the scales used before the 17th century (about 1600) : Dorian D to D. Phrygian E to E. Lydian F to F. Mixolydian G to G. Aeolian A to A. Lochrian B to B. Ionian C to C-the same as our present day C Major scale.

MODO, (I) a mode; as.

MODO MAGGIORE. (I) the Major mode.

MODO MINORE, (I) the minor mode.

MODULATION, the process of passing from one key into another.

MOLL, MINOR G (Dur Major).

MOLTO, much, very. DI MOLTO, very much.

MORCEAU, (F) a musical composition of any kind.

MORDENTE, MORDERE (to bite). A grace consisting of the rapid alternation of the principal note and the note immediately above or below it; and ending on the principal note. Example CDC/CBC. (⬥⬥) (⬥⬥)

MORENDO, dying away and also diminishing the speed.

MOSSO, (I) movement, MENO MOSSO, with less motion.

MOTIF, (G) MOTIV, figure, subject, Leit-motiv.

MOTO, CON (I) with agitation.

MUSETTE, an air in 2/4, 3/4,6/8 time, medium tempo.

MUSIC, the Language of Sounds.

MUTE (DAMPER) (I) (SORDINO) a mechanical device for softening or muffling the tone.

NASAL TONE, in singing this means that the voice is deteriorated by passing through the nostrils.

NATURAL, the character ($\sharp$) that returns a note that has been sharpened or flattened, to its oriiginal state.

NATURAL HARMONY, that produced by the natural and essential chords of the mode.

NINTH, an interval containing an octave and a semitone or tone.

NOBILMENTE, nobly.

NOCTURNE, quiet, reflective piece. Originally Notturno meant a kind of Serenade. Chopin's moods were reflective of the atmosphere of night.

NON, not.

NON TROPPO ALLEGRO, NON TROPPO PRESTO, (I) not too quick.

NOTA, note.

NOTATION, the art of representing musical sounds and their various modivications by notes, signs, terms, etc.

NOTES, are the signs that represent the sounds

ENGLISH	AMERICAN
1. Breve	Double whole-note
2. Semibreve	Whole
3. Minim	1/2
4. Crotchet	1/4
5. Quaver	1/8
6. Semiquaver	1/16
7. Demisemiquaver	1/32
8. Hemidemisemiquaver	1/64

O, (I) or.

OBBLIGATI, OBBLIGATO, (I) necessary.

OBLIQUE, motion between two parts where one ascends or descends, while the other remains stationary.

OBOE, a woodwind instrument, double reed.

OCTAVE, an interval of eight notes.

OFFERTOIRE, (F) OFFERTORY, a part of the Catholic morning service.

OPEN, the strings of an instrument when not pressed are open. This also means the tones produced on such strings. Open notes-on wind instruments, the notes that are proper to the tobe.

OPERA, a musical work sung, drama (tragic and comid) with scenery and acting with accompaniment of an orchestera. (opera Buffa, opera-comique).

P, Abbreviation of piano-soft.

PANTOMINE, (GK) imitation. Musical entertainment so called because it is all mimic.

PARALLEL MOTION, when two parts are moving in the same direction it is said to be in parallel motion.

PARLANDO, PARLANTO, (speaking) the words are sung in a declamatory style.

PARTITA, (G) name given to collections of dance tunes which are played consecutively (suite)

PARTITUR, (G) a score.

PASSING NOTES, notes foreign to the harmony.

PASSIONATO, passionately.

PASTORALE, (1) a dramatic composition (opera) of which the subject is legendary and pastoral in character.

    (2) an instrumental or vocal work in 6/8,9/8,12/8 time. A pastoral (soft) rural movement.

PATETICO, with feeling.

PAUSE, (I. fermata) rest.

PAVAN, PAVANE, PAVIN, slow and solemn dance of 16th and 17th centuries

PEDALE, (I) (pes-a foot) a pedal or stationary bass. In piano the performer presses down the pedal which takes off the dampers.

PERCUSSION, instruments such as drums, tambourines, cymbals, triangles, chimes, glockenspiel, castanets, xylophone.

PERIOD, group of bars.

PESANTE, heavy, applies to whole passages.

PHRASE, one of the smallest among the divisions which distinguish the form of a musical work.

PIANISSIMO, OR PP, (I) extremely soft.

PIANOFORTE, Italian origin called Piano e Forte (soft and loud) a stringed instrument of percussion with keyboard.

PIANO, (I) soft, the opposite of forte.

PIETOSO, pitiful, compassionate.

PIU, (I) as.

PIU LENTO, slower.

PIU MOSSO, increased action.

PIZZACANDO, PIZZICATO, PIZZ, (I) (pinched) pluck string.

PLAGAL, CADENZA, the final tonic chord is preceded by subdominant.

PLUS, (F) more.

POCHETTINO, a very little.

POCHISSMO, the smallest possible.

POCO, a little.

POCO ANIMATO, (I) a little more animated.

POCO ADAGIO, a little slow.

POCO A POCO, by degrees gradually.

POCO A POCO CRESCENDO, louder and louder.

POCO A POCO DIMINUENDO, softer and softer.

POLKA, a well known Bohemian round dance.

POLONAISE, a stately dance originally from poland.

POLYPHONY, is harmonious composition of two or more melodies. In Polyphony one considers the music harizontally. Homophony one considers the music vertically, in structure, etc.

POMPOSO, grand and pompous.

PONTICELLO, the bridge of a string instrument.

PORTAMENTO, (I) the manner of carrying the sound of voice with extreme smoothness from one note to another.

POSITION, means (violin etc.) the places on the finger-board (L. H.) and spaces which the fingers cover in each different shift (position).

PRALLTRILLER, ornament. Inverted mordent (♦♦). A grace formed by the Principal note, above note and returning to the principle note.

PRELUDE, introduction to a main work also a small independent piece.

PREMIERE, (F) first.

PREPARATION, a large proportion of the dissonant combinations in music that delay the movement of a part or voice, are called preparation. (see also suspension).

PRESTISSIMO, very quickly, highest rate of speed in music.

PRESTO, fast.

PRIMO, first, as primo tempo, return to first tempo.

PROGRAMME MUSIC, music is either programme music or absolute music. Programme music usually describes events, moods. (discriptive music, story line, etc.)

PROGRESSION, motion from note to note.

PSALM, a sacred song.

QUADRILLE, (F) a french dance, or a set of five consecutive dance movements.

QUARTER NOTE, a crotchet.

QUARTET, a composition for four instruments or voices.

QUASI, (as if) (I) in the manner or style of; as quasi Allegro, like Allegro.

QUAVER, American eight note.

QUINTET, a composition for five instruments or voices.

R OR R.H., right hand.

RAG TIME, broken rhythm in melody (continuous syncopation)

RALLENTANDO, RITARDANDO, become slow, gradually decreasing speed.

RE, (F) the note D.

REEL, an ancient dance in common time (or 6/4).

REGISTER, the compass of a voice or instrument..

RELATIVE, A Major and minor key which have the same signature (ex.C.M. A m.) are called relative. Ex. A minor is the relative minor of C Major.

RELIGIOSAMENTE, RELIGIOSOS, (I) in a solemn style.

REPLICA, (I) repetition.

REQUIEM, a solemn mass.

RESOLUTION, the process of relieving dissonance by consonance.

REST, the sign of silence.

RETARDATION, a group of discords that resolve upwards.

RHAPSODIE, a composition irregular in form.

RHYTHM, is the distribution of metre, the composition (time, tempi, metre) of the phrase and period.

RIGORE, in most exact time.

RINFORZANDO, RINF, RFZ, increasing in power.

RESOLUTO, resolute.

RITARDANDO, gradually slower.

RITENUTO, (RITENENTE), immediately slow.

RITMICO, rhythmically.

ROMANCE, (F) ROMANZA, (I) a short lyrical piece, simple and elegant.

RONDO, RONDEAU, a piece in which the main theme is always repeated after the introduction of other matter, so as to give a rounded form to the whole.

ROOT, fundamental note of any chord.

RUBATO, (I) robbed (time) the terms tempo rubato are applied when some notes are held longer than their legitimate time, while other are curtailed of their proportonate duration.

SARABAND, a stately dance invented in the 16th century in 3/2 or 3/4 time, begins on the down beat. Later was used in suites.

SAUTILLE, (I) (SALTATO) in violin or violoncello music use skipping motion of bow.

SCALE, (I) (sound-ladder) series of sounds, used in music, arranged step wise in alphabetical order. The Major, minor and chromatic scales are the scales used today. The Major and minor are called diatonic scales.

SCENA, (I) a scene or portion of an opera.

SCHERZANDO, playful, lively, In a light, playful manner.

SCHERZO, (I) (joke, jest) an instrumental composition. bright and often playful or humorous. It is descended from the Minuet and TRio, but is quicker and in ternary form and triple time.

SCHERZOSO, playful.

SCIOLTO, CON SCIOLTEZZA, freely (like ad libitum) but usually applied to longer passages or whole movements.

SCORE, a series of staves on which all the different instrumental or voice parts are written, so that the whole can be read at a glance.

SEC, SECCO (lit. dry) short; staccato.

SECOND, smallest interval in musical scale.

SEGNO, (I) a sign (𝄋) as al segno return to the sign, repeat.

SECULAR MUSIC, music not written for religious purposes.

SEMI, (L) half; as, semitone, half a tone, etc.

SEMIBREVE, a note equal to two minims, whole note.

SEMITONE, a half tone.

SEMIQUAVER, a sixteenth note.

SEMPLICE, SEMPLICEMENTE, SEMPLICITA, CON (I) with simplicity, simple.

SEMPRE, (I) always, SEMPRE FORTE-always loud.

SENZA, (I) without.

SEPTIME, (G) SEPTIEME, (F) the interval of a seventh.

SERENADE, evening song.

SESTA, (I) a sixth.

SETTIMA, (I) a seventh.

SEXTET, a composition for six instruments or voices.

SFORZANDO, SFORZATO, (I) with emphasis and force.

SHAKE OR TRILL, one of the earliest graces. The trill is produced by the regular and rapid repitition of the given note with the note above. The sign is tr

SHARP, the (♯) sharp sign raises a note 1/2 step (semitone).

SI, in solfaring the note B.

SIGNATURE, (1) KEY SIGNATURE, the group of sharps or flats placed at the beginning of the piece and on each (stave) line of music are called the key signature.

(2) TIME SIGNATURE, a sign placed after the clef and key signature which gives the time that the composition is written in.

Ex. 3/4,4/4,3/2, etc)

SIMILAR MOTION, two parts moving in the same direction at the same time.

SIMILE, (I) similarly, in like manner.

SIMPLE, in counterpoint note against note is called simple counterpoint. a more elaborate composition is called figurative counterpoint.

SIXTH, an interval comprising six degrees.

SLARGANDO, SLENTANDO, gradually slower.

SLUR, a curved line drawn over or under a group of notes indicating that all within the slur are to be played Legato. On string instruments in one stroke of the bow; voice-in one breath.

SMORZANDO, dying away.

SOGGETTO, (I) subject or theme.

SOL, the note G.

SOLENNE, solemn.

SOLO, (I) alone (ex. solo voice).

SONATA, a composition of a fairly large scale. Usually in three or four movements. A sonata is written for only one or two instruments. Works that are similar in construction but written for three or four instruments are called Trios, Quartets, Quintets, etc. and if for orchestra, they are called Symphonies.

SONATA FORM, the normal structure is (a) exposition. A first subject, transition, second subject (in the dominant or relative Major). (b) developoment section. (c) recapitulation. The exposition is restated.

SONATINE, a short and easy sonata.

SOPRANO, the highest species of the three classes of female voices. (Contralto, Mezzo-soprano).

SARDINI, (I) mutes, CON SORDINE, with mutes, SENZA CORDINI, without mutes.

SOSTINUTO, SOST., (I) ststained.

SOTTO, (I) under.

SOTTO VOCE, (I) in a soft or subdued manner. (in an undertone).

SPICCATO, distinct and detached manner.

SPIRITO, CON SPIRITOSAMENTE, SPIRITOSO (I) with spirit, animation.

STACCATISSIMO, (I) very detached.

STACCATO, detached from one another by rests.

STAFF, STAVE, lines on which notes are written.

STEM ( ) the line which is drawn fron the head of a note.

STINGUENDO, (I) gradually diminishing the tone.

STOP, the pressure of the fingers on the strings of a violin etc.

STRAIN, a part of a movement divided off by a double bar.

STREPITOSO, noisy, boisterous.

STRETTO, in a fugue, an overlapping of two or more entries of the subject.

STRETTO, STRINGENDO, (I) forcing, accelerating the speed. Gradually faster

SUB, under, below.

SUBDOMINANT, the fourth note of the scale.

SUBITO, suddenly.

SUBJECT, the theme of a movement (musical thought).

SUBMEDIENT, the sixth note of the scale.

SUBTONIC, the seventh note of the scale, a half step below the tonic.

SUITE, a number of pieces grouped together. The classical Suite (Bach, Handel, etc,) consisted of a number of dances in Binary Form, Allemande, Courante, Sarabande, Bouree Minuet, and Gigue were some of the dances used in suites.

SUL, (I) on or upon.

SUPERTONIC, the second note of the scale, the note above the tonic.

SUSPENSION, occurs when the conjunct motion of the parts are stopped while the rest of the components of the chord proceed one step onwards, and therefore represent a different root.

SUSTAINED, notes sustained throughout their whole power and length.

SWELL, the part of the organ that consists of numerous pipes enclosed in a box, connect by a pedal by which it may gradually open or shut and thus the tone made lower by degrees.

SYMPHONY, a orchestra composition, similar in structure to the Sonant, but usually in four movements.

SYNCOPATIION, connecting one unaccented note with the following accented one, in the same bar or different bar, rorming a continual sound.

TAMBOURIN, (F) an old French dance in duble time, accompanied by a small drum called the tabor.

TANGO, a dance of Mexican origin.

TANTO, (I) as much, so much.

TARANTELLA, a quick Italian daance in 6/8 time.

TEMPO, (pace) the degree of movement.

TEMPO PRIMO, (I) indicates a return to first tempo.

TENOR, highest natural voice of men.

TENTH, interval of an octave and a third.

TENUTE, TENUTO, TEN. (I) held, sustained for full time.

TENZ, (G) TERZA, (I) the interval of a third.

THEME, (F. THEME) (I. MOTIV) a subject.

THIRD, an interval of three degrees.

THIRTEENTH, an interval of an octave and a sixth.

THOROUGH BASS, continues without a break.

TIES, curved lines drawn over notes.

TIMBRE, (F) tone colour, quality.

TIME, the time is given in the signature. The denominator gives the component, time units. (what size note gets a beat (time unit)). The numerator tells us how many beats in a bar.

TIMPANI OR TYMPANI, (I) the kettle drums.

TIRE, (F) down stroke of the bow. (in string music.)

TOOCATA, (I) (to touch). A composition for a key board instrument in the style of improvisation and designed to show off the dexterity of the performer.

TONALITY, is the character of a composition by virtue of the following: Tonality rest mainly on the relation of its tones, chords to its key note, or tonic and the balance of tonal harmonies, related and leading chords.

TONE, (I) scientificaly a musical note free from harmonics a tone consists of a fundamental and a series of harmonic overtones.

      (2) also means quality.

TONIC, the name given to the keynote from which the key of the piece is named.

TONLEITER, (G) the scale.

TRANQUILLO, TRANQUILLAMENTE, TRANQUILLITA, CON, TRANQUILLEZZA, CON, (I) with tranquility.

TRANSITION, (modulation) passage from one key to another in a regular manner.

TRANSPOSITION, changing the piece into another key from that in which it is written.

TRE, three.

TRE CORD, (lit. three strings) release the left (soft) pedal of the pianoforte.

TREMOLO, (I) rapid reiteration of a single note (string etc.) or chord (pianoforte) without regard to any time value.

TRES, (F) very.

TRIAD, a chord of three consisting of a bottom note, third and fifth.

TRIANGLE, percussion instrument consisting of a steel rod in triangular shape and a metal beater.

TRILL, see shake.

TRIO, a composition for three instruments or voices.

TRIPLET, a group of three notes arising from the division of a note into three equal parts and marked with the figure 3 over the middle note.

TROMBA, (I) a triplet.

TROMBONE, a powerful wind instrument with a sliding tube.

TROPPO, (I) too much. Adagio non troppo, not too slow.

TROUBADOURS, early poet-musicians of Provinces.

TRUMPET, wind instrument (transposing) usually of brass.

TUBA, a wind instrument, the lowest or bass instrument in the wind (brass) orchestra section.

TUNE, a succession of measured sounds. (A formalised melody).

TUNING-FORK, (pitch carrier) used to accurately (measure of pitch) tune instruments.

TURN, an embellishment, consisting of the note on which the turn is made, the note above it, and the semitone below it (ex. CDCBC-???)

TUTTA, TUTTE, TUTTI, TUTTO, (I) all. Tutti expresses the entrance of all the instruments before or after a solo.

TUTTA FORZE, (I) as loud as possible.

TYMPANI, (TIMPANI) the kettle drums.

UN, UNA, UNO, one.

UN PEU, UN POCO, a little.

UNA CORDA, (I) (one string) the left pedal of pianoforte shift's the action to the right therefore the hammers strike two strings instead of the three usually struck. T. C. tre corde. Tutte le corde returns to the use of three strigs.

UND, (G) and.

UNIS, UNISON, two sounds of same pitch.

UN POCO RITENUTO, gradually slower.

V, is used by the Italians as an abbreviation of the word violin. (also VL).

VALSE, see Waltz.

VALUE, length of notes in respect to time.

VARIATIONS, ornamented repetitions, or various combinations of a theme or part with various embellishments or changes in rhythm, harmony or key.

VELOCE, swiftly, CON VELOCITA, (I) in a rapid time.

VESPERS, the evening services in the Catholic church.

VIBRATE, (I) Vibrating, (to vibrate) pulsation of a note by slight, rapid recurring changes of pitch.

VIF, lively, quick.

VIGOROS, vigorous.

VIOLA, (alto) a stringed instrument, intermediate in size and compass between the violin and violoncello.

VIOLIN, (treble) a stringed instrument (foour strings). One of four sizes: treble (violin) alto (viola) tenor (violoncello) bass (cpmtrabass).

VIOLONCELLO, (tenor) a stringed instrument.

VIRGINAL, VIRGINALS, keyboard instrument (1500-1700).

VIRTUOSO, one who has greatest mastery over his art, instrument or singing.

VIVACE, VIVACEMENTE, quick and lively.

VIVO, see Vivace.

VOCAL, music composed for the voice.

VOCE, (I) the voice.

VOICE, sounds produced by the vocal organs in singing soprano, mezzosoprano, contralto, alto, tenor, bariton, bass-baritone, bass.

VOLANTE, flying.

VOLTA, time.

VOLTI, VOLTI SUBITO, V.S., turn over quickly V.S. (turn page).

VOX, (L) voice.

WALTZ, a dance originating in Germany, the music of which is usually in 3/4 measure.

WENIG, (G) little.

WHOLE NOTE, a semibreve.

WIND INSTRUMENTS, all instruments the sound of which are produced by the lungs of the players, or by the wind of bellows.

WOHLTEMPERIRTE CLAVIER, DAS, the well-tempered Clavier (48 Preludes and fugues) in two parts, covers all the Major and minor keys was written by Johann Sebastian BAch in 1722-1744.

XYLOPHONE, a percussion instrument, series of wood bars, sounded by striking with two small wooden hammers, written on one treble stave and at actual pitch.

ZART. (G) tender.

ZEITMASS, (G) speed, tempo.

ZITHER, (G) of the family of string instruments plucked with a plectrum, developed from the cither.

ZU, (G) too.

Compiled by, Herman J. Daldin

September 5, 1995..........

Printed in the United States
By Bookmasters